Kevin was digging in the soil. He was looking for his bone, but he found a yellow toy trumpet.

He dug it up out of the soil. He shook it. Little clumps of soil fell out of it. Then Kevin ran around with the yellow toy trumpet in his mouth.

He was enjoying himself, when all of a sudden, … ta-raa, ta-raa, ta-rum. Oh no! A funny noise came out of the yellow toy trumpet.

Kevin liked the funny noise. Ta-raa, ta-raa, ta-rum. But Wellington did not like it. He was annoyed. The noise had spoiled his sleep.

Kevin was a bad boy! Wellington barked at him. Kevin dropped the toy trumpet. He sat down in a sulk. Wellington had spoiled his fun.

Wellington went back to sleep. Kevin picked up the yellow toy trumpet. He took it to the wood. Now he would enjoy himself blowing the trumpet.

He pointed the yellow toy trumpet up to the sky and he blew down it.

TA-RAA ... TA-RAA ... TA-RUM. It made a very loud noise. Kevin loved it.

But the noise annoyed an owl. It spoiled his daytime sleep. He flew down from his tree and he took the yellow toy trumpet out of Kevin's mouth.

Then the owl flew over the pond. He dropped the yellow toy trumpet into the deep water. Kevin was annoyed. The owl had spoiled his fun.

So he ran around singing, " owww ... owwww " and the noise he made was worse than the trumpet! What could the owl and Wellington do now?

"oi"	"oy"
soil	toy
noise	enjoy
spoiled	annoyed
pointed	boy
	enjoying